MAZE

Vol 13

Ages 4-6

FOR KIDS

MAZE BOOK

SOCIAL MEDIA

- **f** /MySweetBooks1
- **Twitter** /MySweetBooks1
- **Instagram** /MySweetBooks1
- **Pinterest** /MySweetBooks

Email Us : mysweetbooks1@gmail.com

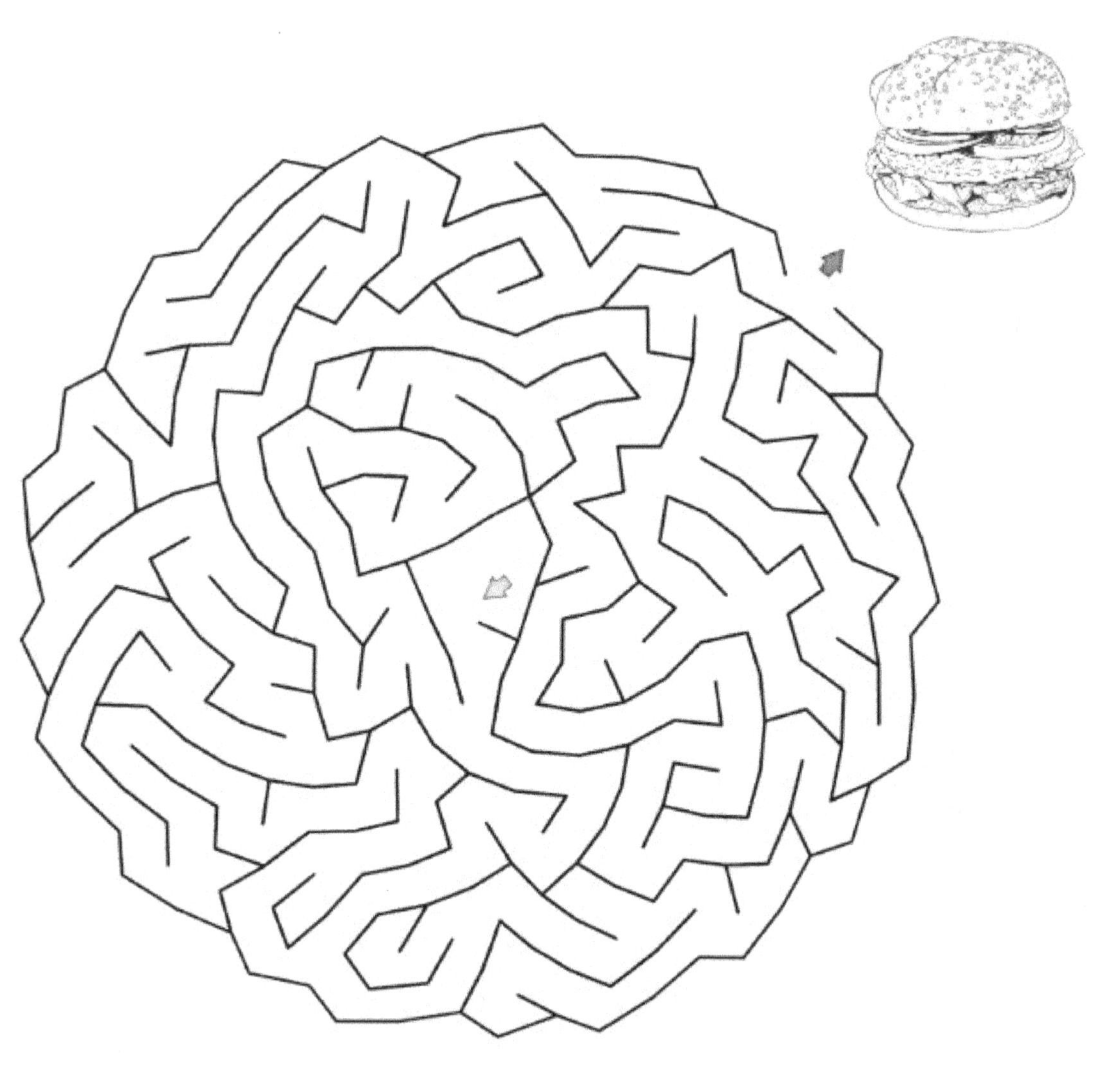

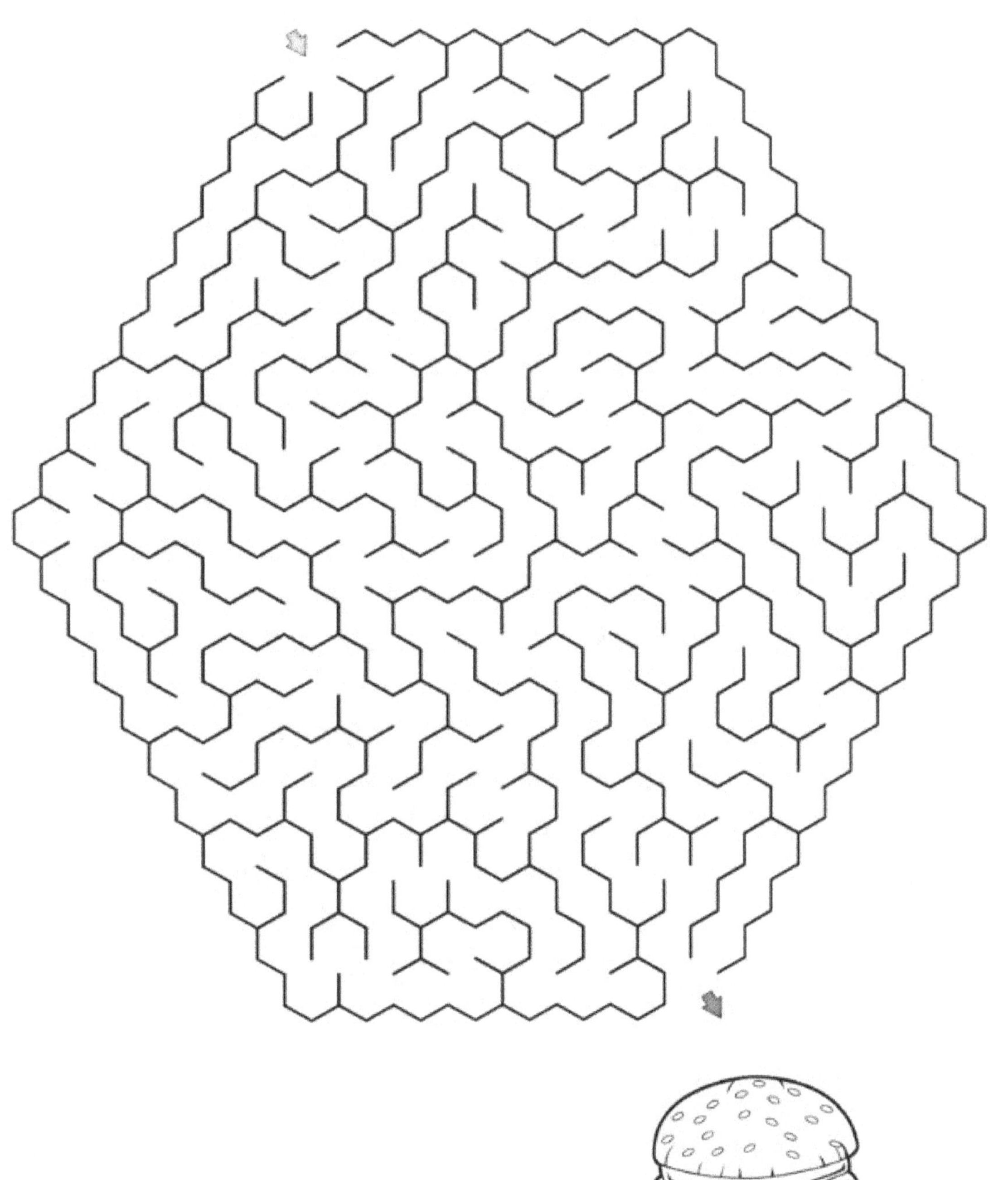

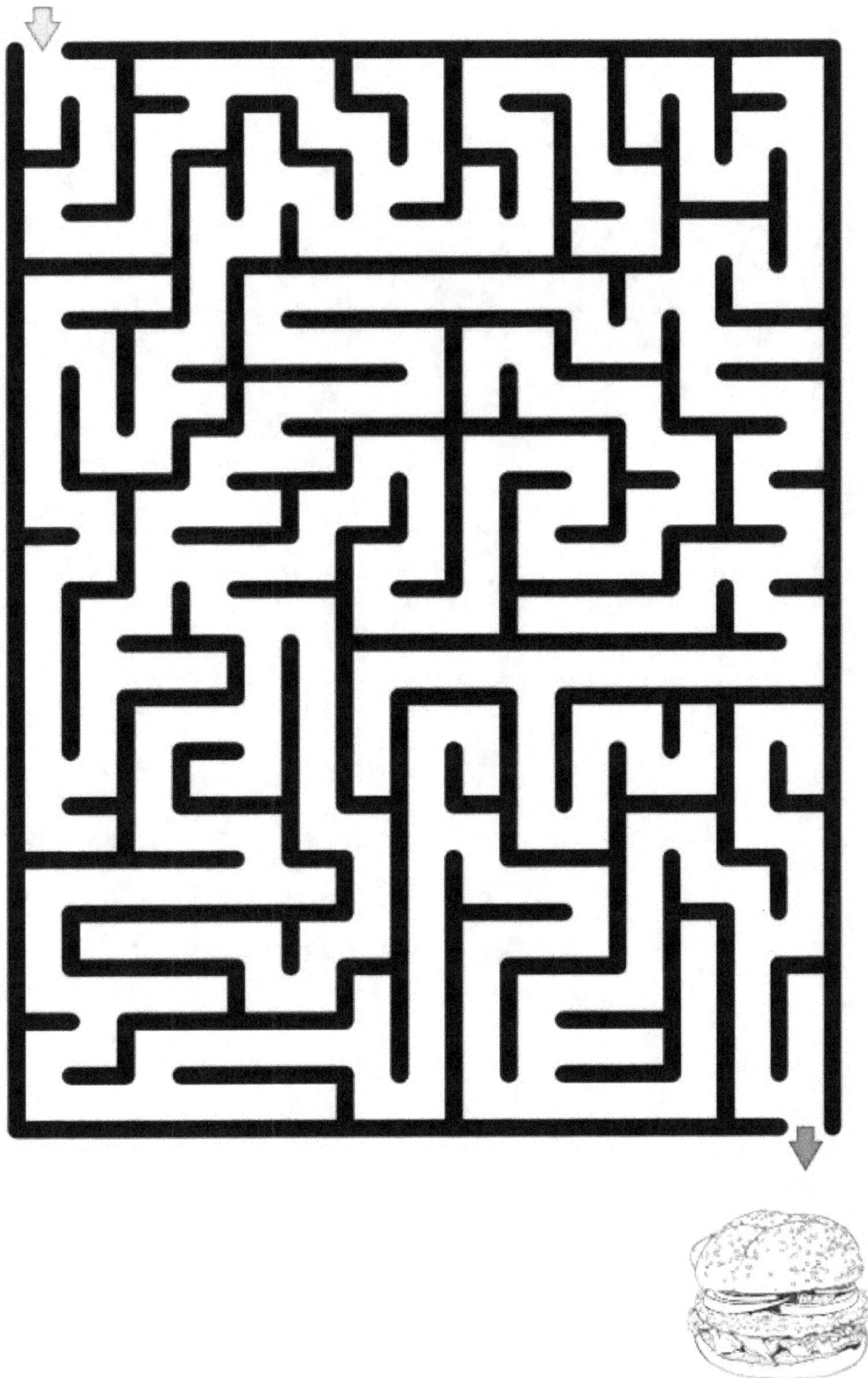

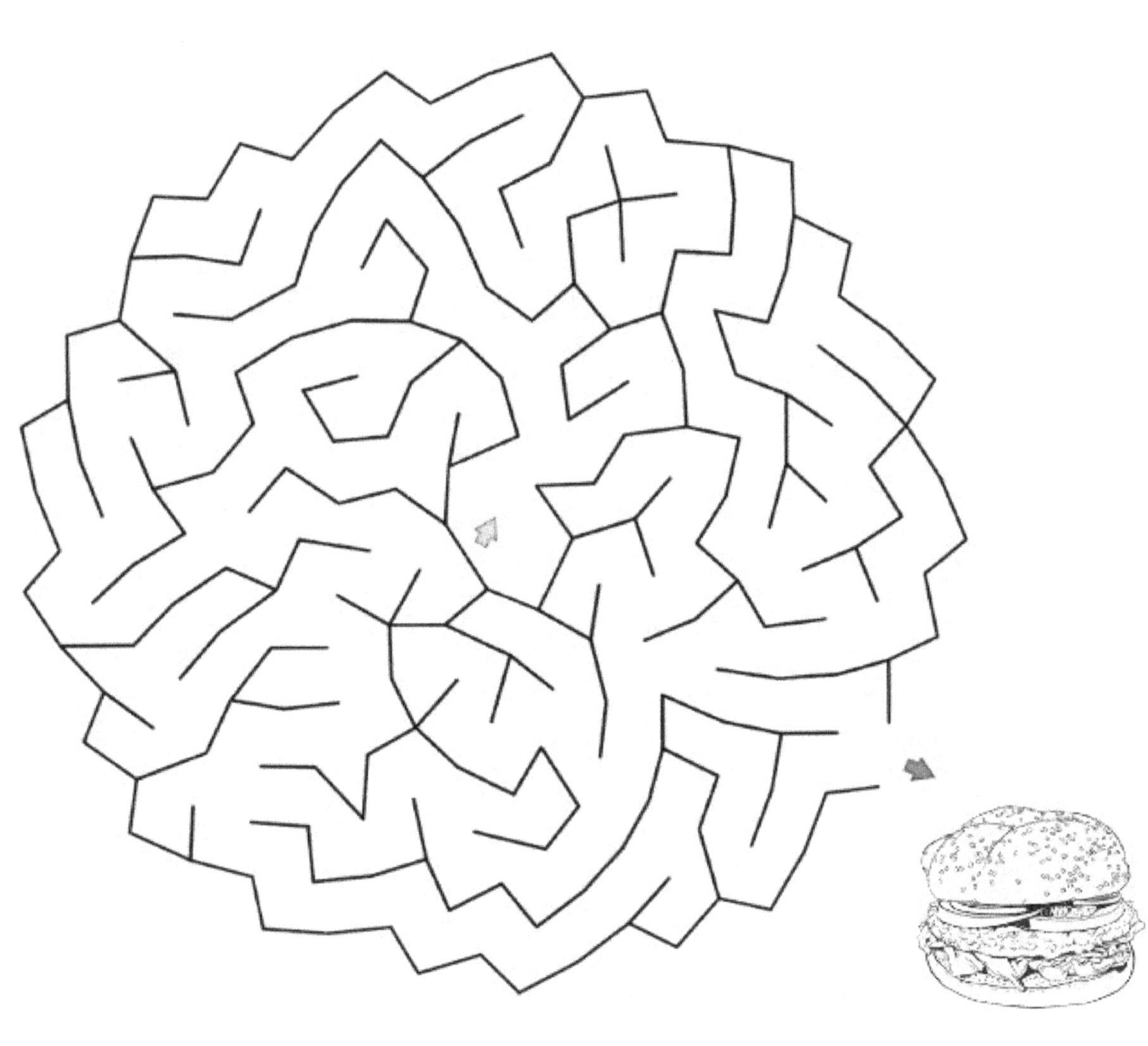

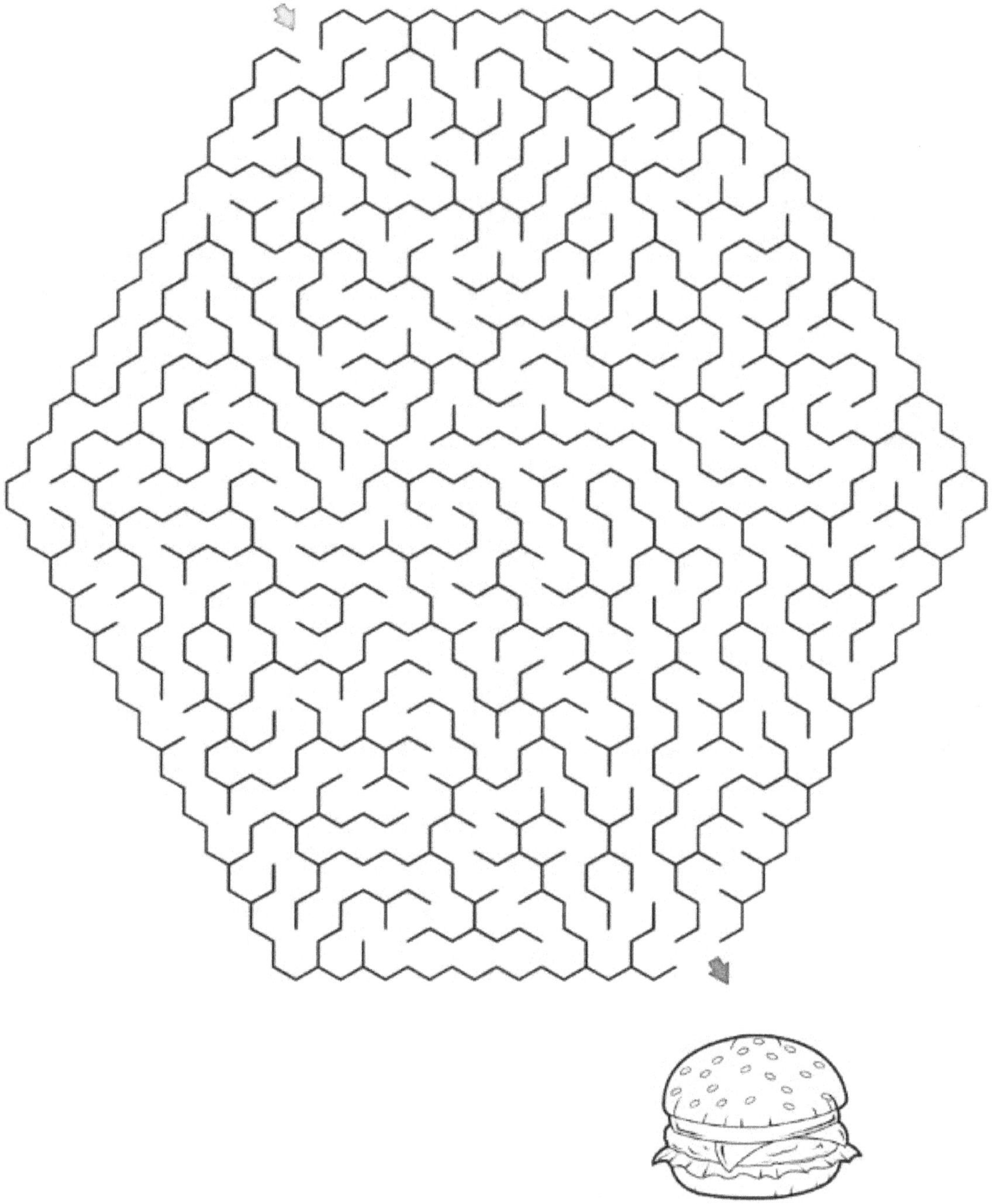

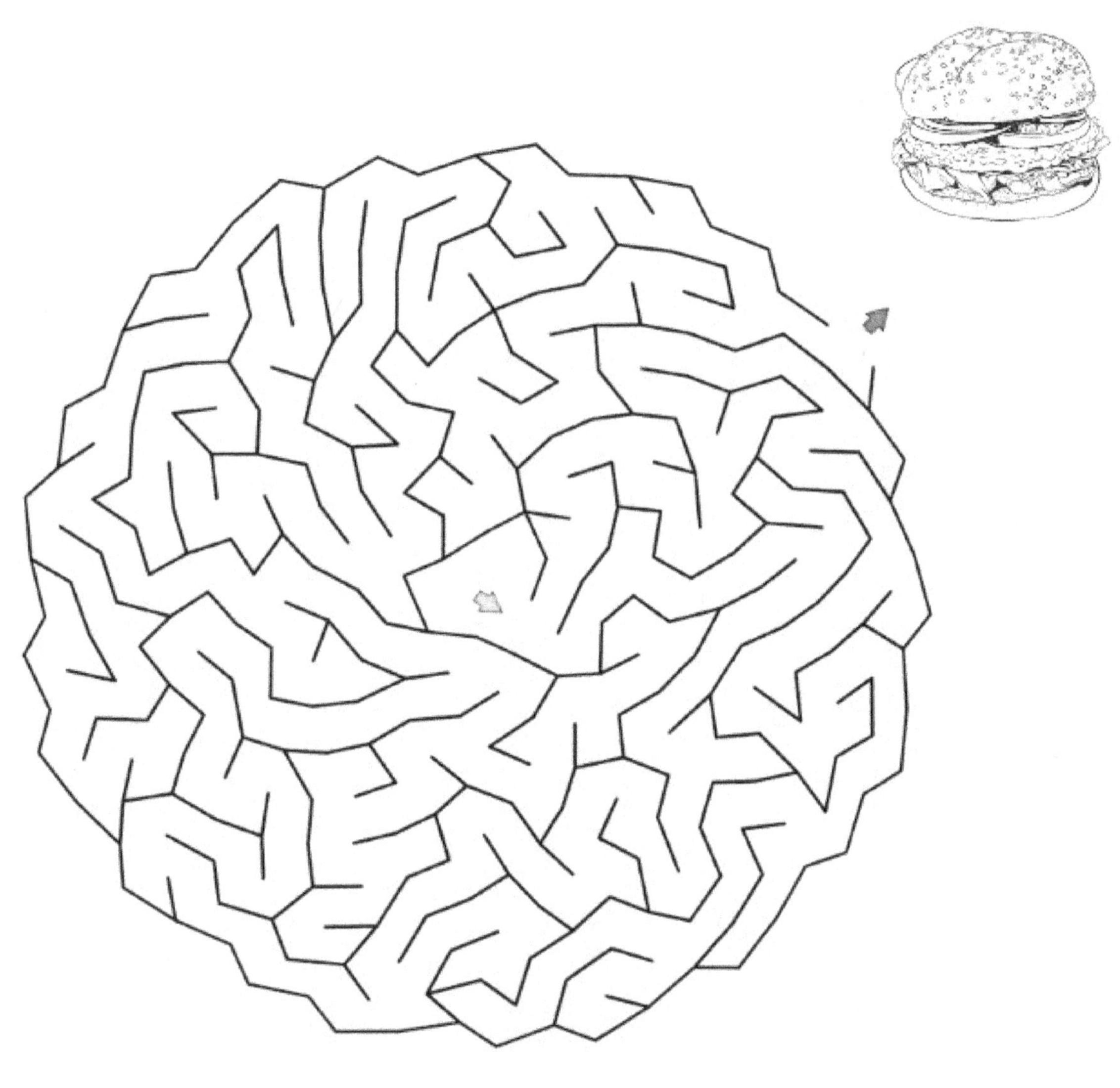

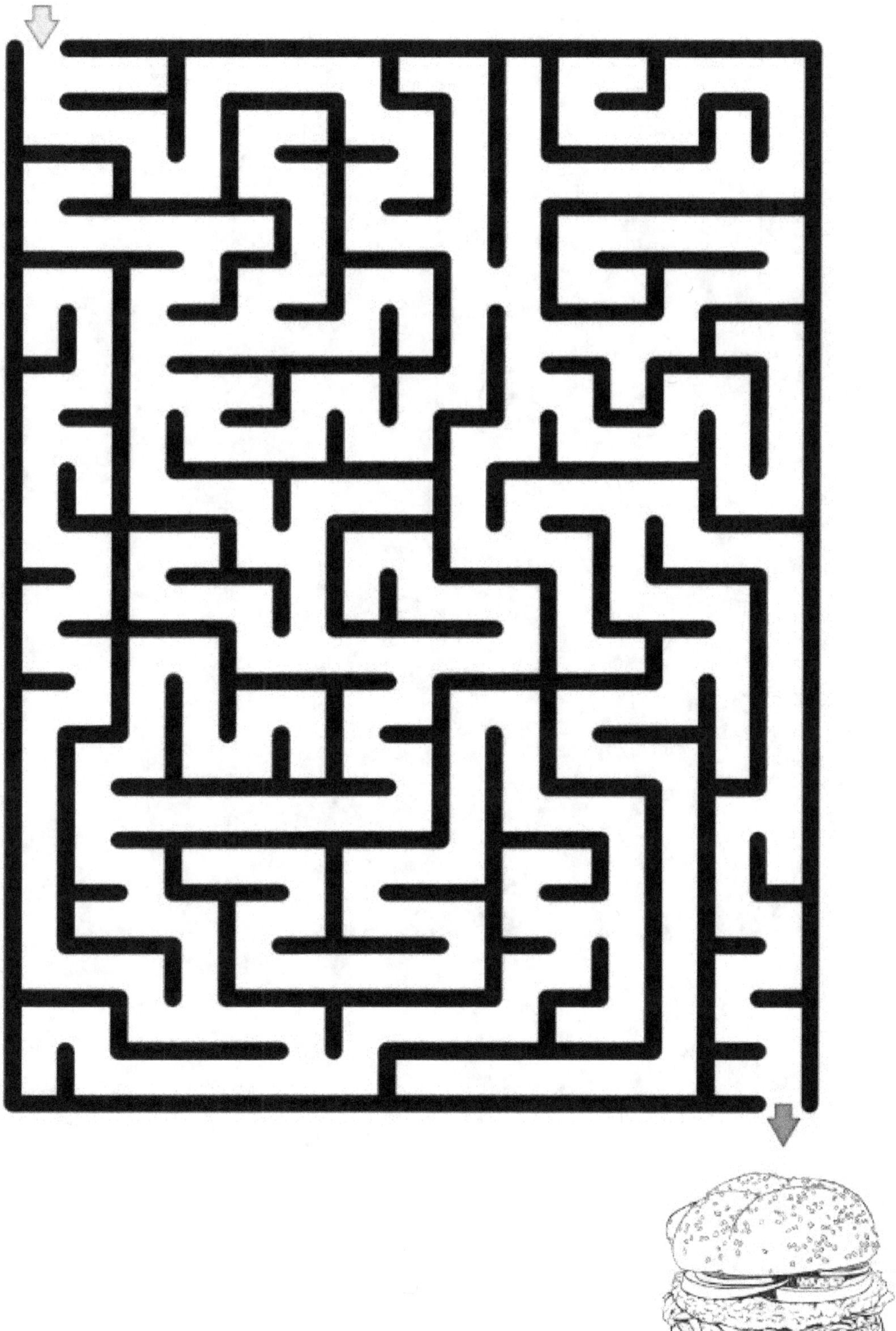

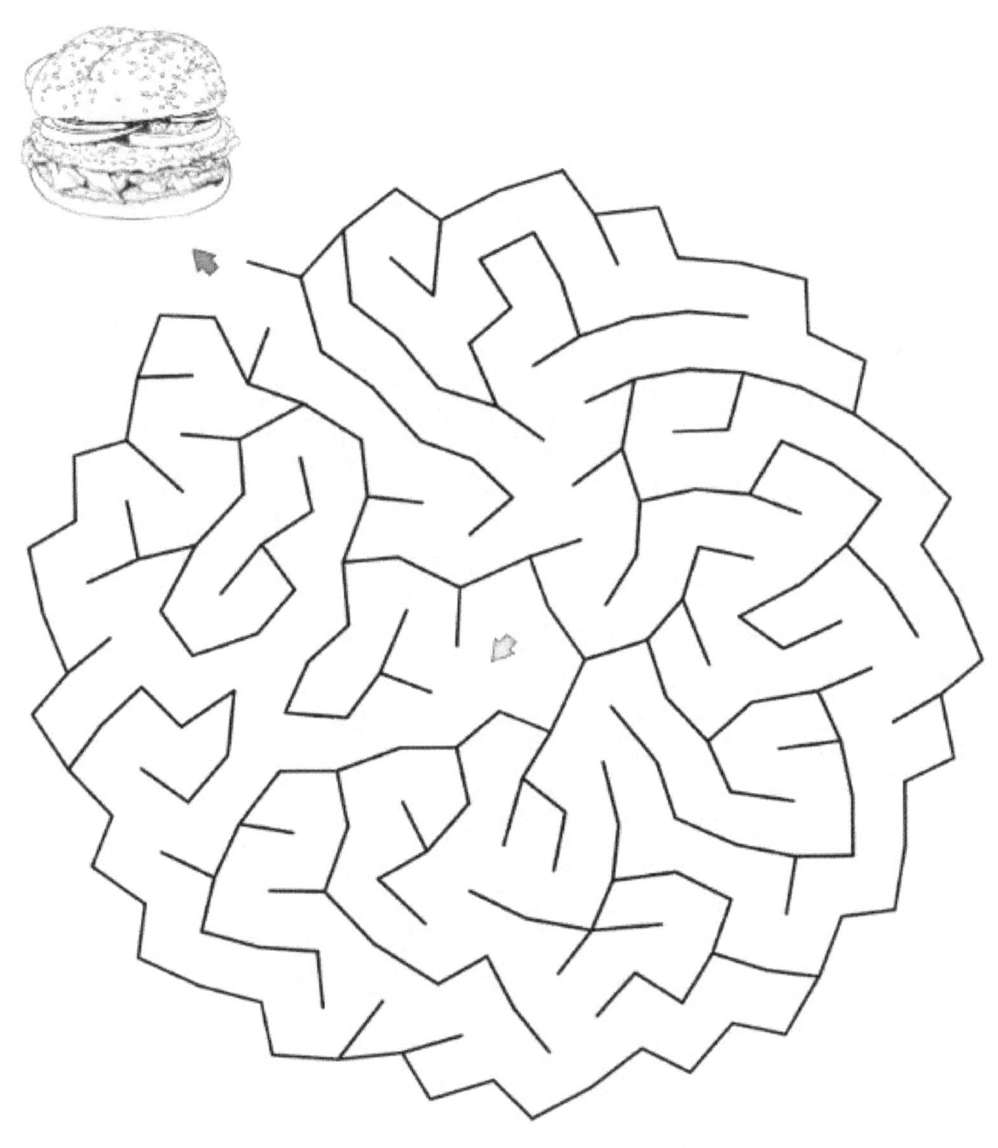

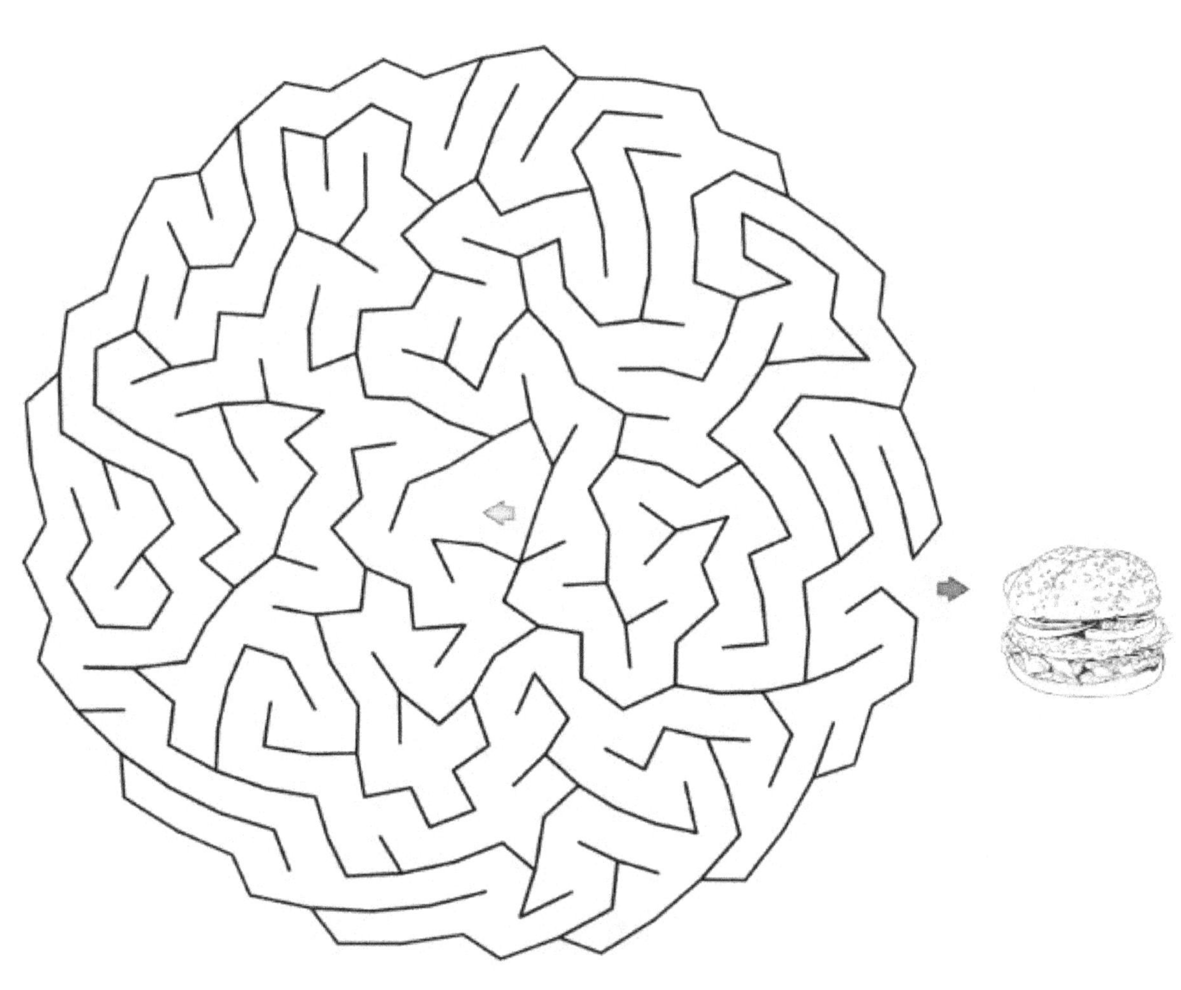

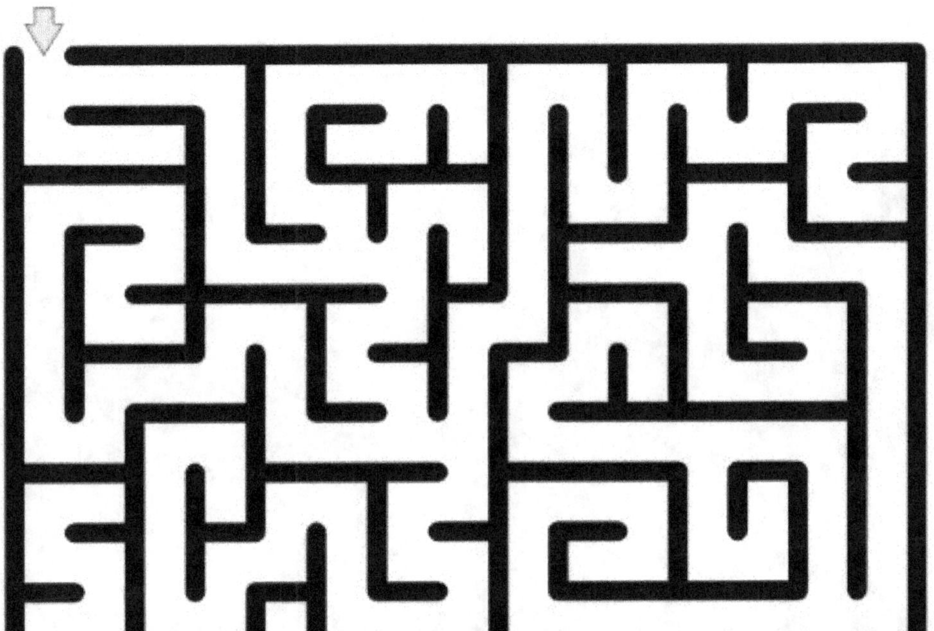